Classic Recipes of
GREECE

Classic Recipes of GREECE

TRADITIONAL FOOD AND COOKING
IN 25 AUTHENTIC DISHES

RENA SALAMAN

LORENZ BOOKS

This edition is published by
Lorenz Books,
an imprint of Anness Publishing Ltd,
108 Great Russell Street, London
WC1B 3NA

www.lorenzbooks.com;
www.annesspublishing.com

© Anness Publishing Limited 2014

If you like the images in this book and
would like to investigate using them for
publishing, promotions or advertising,
please visit our website
www.practicalpictures.com for more
information.

Publisher: Joanna Lorenz
Editor: Helen Sudell
Designer: Nigel Partridge
Production Controller: Mai-Ling Collyer
Recipe Photography: Martin Brigdale

The image on the front cover is of Fried
Squid page 28.

A CIP catalogue record for this book is
available from the British Library

PUBLISHER'S NOTE
Although the advice and information in this
book are believed to be accurate and true
at the time of going to press, neither the
authors nor the publisher can accept any
legal responsibility or liability for any errors
or omissions that may have been made nor
for any inaccuracies nor for any loss, harm
or injury that comes about from following
instructions or advice in this book.

Printed and bound in China

PUBLISHER'S ACKNOWLEDGMENTS
The Publisher would like to thank the
following agencies for the use of their
images. Alamy: p9, p10tr, p11tr. Fotalia: p6.

COOK'S NOTES
Bracketed terms are intended for American
readers. For all recipes, quantities are given
in both metric and imperial measures and,
where appropriate, in standard cups and
spoons. Follow one set of measures, but
not a mixture, because they are not
interchangeable.

Standard spoon and cup measures are
level. 1 tsp = 5ml, 1 tbsp = 15ml, 1 cup =
250ml/8fl oz. Australian standard
tablespoons are 20ml. Australian readers
should use 3 tsp in place of 1 tbsp for
measuring small quantities.

American pints are 16fl oz/2 cups.
American readers should use 20fl oz/2.5
cups in place of 1 pint when measuring
liquids.

Electric oven temperatures in this book are
for conventional ovens. When using a fan
oven, the temperature will probably need to
be reduced by about 10–20°C/20–40°F.
Since ovens vary, you should check with
your manufacturer's instruction book for
guidance.

The nutritional analysis given for each
recipe is calculated per portion (i.e. serving
or item), unless otherwise stated. If the
recipe gives a range, such as Serves 4–6,
then the nutritional analysis will be for the
smaller portion size, i.e. 6 servings. The
analysis does not include optional
ingredients, such as salt added to taste.

Medium (US large) eggs are used unless
otherwise stated.

Contents

Introduction

From the fertile pastures and hillside vineyards of mainland Greece to its sun-drenched islands, a flavoursome diet has developed, centred on vegetables and other fresh ingredients, and with quality seasonal produce being of utmost importance. It is an ancient cuisine that has been passed from generation to generation, keeping the old traditions alive. Greek food is also wonderfully healthy: it is the classic Mediterranean diet, rich in fruit and vegetables, with a little meat and fish, olives and olive oil, home-made bread, and local cheeses.

Left: Greek fishing boats line up in the harbour at Hydra Port, the only town on the island of Hydra.

Greek Cuisine

Greek food is mostly based on a rural tradition – on recipes that have been passed down by word of mouth and from mother to daughter. Cooking and eating together is central to Greek family life and eating outdoors is a great pleasure during the summer months. Traditional country homes have their ovens outside to keep the house cool. These external ovens are lit only once a day, for bread and meat or pies. In more basic households, a pot will be placed over a fire to cook a stewed dish or soup.

Below: Freshly made vegetable dips, olives and pitta are popular meze fare all over Greece.

Above: Coffee and sweet pastries are often taken as a mid-morning break.

Daily life

The day starts with a light breakfast, and may be simply a small cup of Greek coffee or tea with lemon. By mid-morning many Greeks enjoy a snack such as *koulouri*, covered with sesame seeds, or a hot cheese pie, called *tyropitta*, bought from a street seller. Lunch is traditionally served late – around 2 p.m. – although many of the younger generation now eat at about midday. Cakes and pastries are an afternoon treat taken with coffee. The main meal of the day is taken later in the evening with the whole family.

Most family meals start with a meze table, filled with local specialities and tzatsiki, hummus, taramasalata, fried shellfish, cured meats or fish, rissoles, aubergine (eggplant) salads, pitta and plenty of crusty white bread. The main meal of either marinated lamb, or fresh fish, is often barbecued outside in the spring and summer, served with salads and breads. During the colder months, large pots of moussaka or pork gently stewed with orange and chickpeas, or chicken with avgolemono sauce, are prepared in an oven.

Right: Grilled halloumi cheese and fresh salad will be part of any meze table.

Greek Food and Festivals

In Greece 98 per cent of the population follow the Greek Orthodox faith, and celebrate numerous saints' days and festivals throughout the year.

Easter

The highlight of the Greek Orthodox calendar is Easter Sunday but there are also plenty of festivities ahead of eating the traditional roast lamb. Three weeks before Lent is *apokries* (Carnival), when the Greeks eat meat in preparation for the Lenten fasts. During the first week of Carnival a pig is slaughtered, and people can

Below: The traditional Easter bread, complete with red eggs.

eat as much meat as they like in the second week. During the third week cheese is eaten.

The first day of Lent is known as Clean Monday, the day on which to clean all pots and pans to make sure that no trace of animal produce remains. The Clean Monday feast consists of food where no meat, butter, eggs or cheese are present and ushers in 40 days of fasting. Families picnic on locally caught shellfish, taramasalata, hummus, octopus, salads, pickles and loaves of unleavened bread.

On the Thursday before Easter traditional red-dyed eggs are made (the red dye symbolizing Christ's blood). These brightly coloured eggs are displayed in cake shops and are also added to the Easter bread which is made from braided sweet dough formed into a plait or circle.

On Easter Sunday the red-dyed eggs are cracked open to celebrate new life. The highlight of the day, however is

Above: A Greek woman holds a tray of baked Easter biscuits.

the whole lamb gently roasting outside on a spit. Sometimes, stuffed lamb or goat that has been cooked overnight will be brought to the feast instead of spit-roast lamb. The tables are set outside and laid with white tablecloths, spring flowers and plates of salads and bread. The men drink retsina and ouzo while they watch the lambs roasting.

Afterwards, there will be sweets made with the first

cheeses of the season as well as cinnamon-flavoured pastries and special Easter biscuits to celebrate the end of Lent. The day concludes with dancing and drinking.

Christmas

In Greece, Christmas is less significant than Easter, although it is a national holiday and still involves plenty of feasting, dancing and celebrations, including the giving of presents. The Christmas table is filled with all sorts of food. Traditionally, roast piglet or another pork dish is eaten for the main meal. There is always meat (pork mainly, or turkey) and *Christopsomo* (Christ's bread). The meal is followed by a range of traditional sweets, *diples* (fried dough cookies dipped in honey) and *melomakarona* (honey-dipped cookies, often stuffed with nuts). Sweets, cakes and Christmas cookies are all given out as gifts to the children throughout the festive period.

New Year

The national holiday of Saint Basil is on 1 January. As it coincides with New Year, the holiday is celebrated by eating the traditional Basil cake. This is actually a glazed bread, called *vasilopita*, with a coin hidden inside; whoever finds the coin will enjoy good fortune in the coming year.

To celebrate fertility and the hope of good fortune in the New Year, Greeks eat symbolic foods, including almonds, pomegranates, honey and sesame seeds.

Above: The local baker cuts up the name bread to hand out to celebrating children.

Name days

Traditionally, Greek children do not celebrate their birthdays after the age of 12. Instead they celebrate the saint after whom they were named. Each saint has a special day and celebrations take place all over the country. Friends and relatives call on the named person, bringing all kinds of cakes and pastries, and a special bread is baked.

Classic Ingredients

The Mediterranean sea and sun-drenched soil of Greece provides a rich variety of fresh ingredients for the home cook.

Meat and poultry

Most meat recipes are for lamb and few include beef. Pork is also enjoyed, although less frequently than lamb. For Sunday roasts, a leg of lamb will usually be chosen over any other cut. The traditional lemon and egg sauce, *avgolemono*, will often be served with the meat. Cut into cubes, lamb is also simmered with vegetables, oregano, thyme and garlic in a

Below: Squid can be cooked whole or sliced before grilling.

casserole. Souvlakia are kebabs that make tasty street food, where they are sold in soft pitta bread with a yogurt, garlic and cucumber dressing.

Most poultry is free-range and full of flavour. Long, slow cooking methods are traditionally used so that the meat will be tender and moist.

Fish and seafood

As 90 per cent of Greeks live close to or by the sea, seafood has a special place in this cuisine. The favoured cooking methods are simply baking, frying or grilling (broiling) with olive oil, lemon juice and a few herbs. Small oily fish, such as sardines and mackerel are often wrapped in vine leaves before barbecuing. This helps to seal in the flavour. Anchovies are especially popular in Greece, and are eaten fresh as well as salted or marinated in olive oil. Other fish that are readily available include conger eel, red mullet, tuna and swordfish. Cephalopods are also eaten, particularly on the islands.

Squid is often fried and served with cannellini bean soup for a filling dish. Tiny squid are sweet and tender and are usually eaten whole. The flesh of cuttlefish is normally fried but it can also be slow-cooked with white wine and onions. Octopus is either cooked with red wine or served raw with olive oil and lemon. Shellfish are traditionally chargrilled or pan-fried with herbs, olive oil and lemon juice.

Olives and olive oil

Eaten as part of a meze, made into bread and cooked with many dishes, olives are abundantly used in Greek cuisine. The best-quality olives are marinated in extra virgin olive oil with fresh and dried herbs. The black Kalamata olive is the best known. The quality of Greek's olive oil is exceptional and is used daily, with the average person consuming 20 litres (35 pints) of oil per year.

Right: Greek olives are known throughout the world as being of the highest quality.

Above: Feta cheese is the most popular cheese in Greece.

Dairy

Goats and sheep provide most of the dairy produce in Greece, and their cheeses and yogurts are famous for their exceptional quality. Feta is made from sheep's milk and is a staple ingredient. It is used in salads, baked in pies and crumbled over omelettes. Other popular Greek cheeses include Halloumi, which is a firm cheese that is often fried or grilled (broiled) and served with fresh green leaves; Kasseri, which is a semi-hard cheese made from sheep's milk, and is often eaten on its own or with fruit; and Graviera, which is a hard cheese. It has a mild flavour and is normally used for grating over pasta.

Thick and creamy Greek yogurt is delicious combined with honey and walnut for breakfast; served alongside stuffed vegetables, such as *dolmades*; made into a rich, chilled soup with cucumber and mint; or to make a sweet yogurt cake called *yiaourtopitta*.

Vegetables

In Greece the diet is centred on seasonal vegetables and a trip to the local market to choose fresh produce is a way of life for all Greeks. Vegetables are served in small dishes in the same way as mezedes. They are also stuffed, baked, grilled, added to stews, or made into soups, and no meal is complete without a salad of fresh leaves. Aubergines (eggplants) are the essential ingredient in the famous moussaka, where they are layered with minced lamb and a rich cheese sauce. Courgettes (zucchini) are a popular summer vegetable, often coated in seasoned flour

Above: Aubergines are often fried in olive oil and served cold.

and fried or stuffed as a meze. Tomatoes grow in abundance in Greece and are used to add colour and flavour to salads and sauces. Okra is often cooked with onions and tomatoes or they can be dusted with flour and fried.

The Greeks enjoy a salad with every meal. It can be simply *horta* – green leaves dressed with oil and lemon juice – or it can include a variety of vegetables. *Horiatiki salata* is a peasant-style salad, which includes tomatoes, onion, pepper, olives, feta cheese and fresh oregano and is perfect with grilled fish for a light lunch.

Herbs

In Greece several varieties of herbs can be gathered wild from the hillsides and taken home to be used in cooking. Although parsley and oregano are the most commonly used herbs, fennel grows wild and is also used to flavour stews. Another hillside herb, thyme, is added to fish and meat and is especially fragrant when partnered with oregano. Whole bunches of dill are a key component of the classic Greek dish of cubed lamb, cos lettuce and the lemon and egg sauce *avgolemono*. Flat-leaf parsley, mint, basil and garlic are also all widely used.

Below: The herb oregano adds flavour to many dishes.

Fruits

With its wonderful climate, fruit grows abundantly in Greece and many kinds are available for eating fresh, cooking or making into preserves. Oranges are used in savoury as well as sweet dishes. Nectarines are made into preserves, and kumquats are candied and also made into a rich liqueur.

The lemon holds a special place in Greek hearts and is a familiar combination with olive oil for a salad dressing, and with eggs in the sauce *avgolemono*. The lemon blossom can also be made into a preserve.

The quince ripens in October and is delicious baked with lamb in casseroles. It also makes a lovely sauce with olive oil, garlic and onion to serve with pork.

Grapevines are a familiar sight in the Greek countryside and apart from their use in wine, grapes are eaten fresh to follow a meal, and their must – the crushed fruit after it has been pressed for winemaking – can be mixed with semolina to make a dessert called *moustalevria*.

Spoon sweets

As the different fruits ripen during the year they are made into sweet preserves known as spoon sweets, so-called because they are eaten from a spoon. They are usually served with a glass of water. Dried fruits, such as apricots and raisins, can also be used. Some preserves are especially delicious: kumquats with their exquisite oil are excellent. Cherry tomatoes, although a vegetable fruit, make a delicious preserve combined with quince, and many fruit preserves make a luscious topping for yogurt and honey.

Food of the Gods

Think of Greece, and your mouth positively waters: all those wonderful and diverse flavours, combined so skilfully in a cuisine that is good for your heart, body and soul. The essence of Greek cuisine is its simplicity – the dishes may sometimes be frugal but they are always appetizing. From fresh salad leaves tossed in extra virgin olive oil and lemon juice, and colourful swordfish skewers; to slow-cooked lamb casserole, richly flavoured with thyme and garlic, and sweetly spiced walnut cake, this collection of recipes will reveal all that is good about this homely but never dull cuisine.

Left: The Greek word mezedes *means 'a tableful' and it comes from the Middle Eastern tradition of sharing small portions of savoury foods with family and friends.*

Chicken Soup with Egg and Lemon Sauce
Kotopoulo soupa avgolemono

Serves 4–6

1 chicken, about 1.6kg/3½ lb
1.75 litres/3 pints/7½ cups water
2 onions, halved
2 carrots
3 celery sticks, each sliced into 3–4
  pieces
a few flat-leaf parsley sprigs
3–4 black peppercorns
50g/2oz/generous ⅓ cup short
  grain rice
salt
lemon quarters, to serve

For the egg and lemon sauce

5ml/1 tsp cornflour (cornstarch)
2 large (US extra large) eggs, at room
  temperature
juice of 1–2 lemons

1 Place the chicken in a large pan with the water. Bring to the boil and skim using a slotted spoon until the surface of the liquid is clear. Add the vegetables, parsley and peppercorns, season with salt and bring to the boil. Lower the heat slightly, then cover the pan and cook for 1 hour until the chicken is very tender.

2 Carefully lift out the chicken and put it on a board. Strain the stock and set it aside, but discard the vegetables. Pull away the chicken breasts, skin them and dice the flesh. Do the same with the legs. Pour the stock back into the pan and add the chicken meat.

3 Shortly before serving, heat the stock and diced chicken. When the stock boils, add the rice. Cover the pan and cook for about 8 minutes, until soft. Take the pan off the heat and let the soup cool a little before adding the sauce.

4 Make the sauce. Mix the cornflour to a paste with a little water. Beat the eggs in a bowl, add the lemon juice and the cornflour mixture and beat together until smooth. Gradually beat a ladleful of the chicken stock into the egg mixture, then continue to beat for 1 minute. Add a second ladleful in the same way. By now the sauce will be warm so you can pour it slowly into the soup, and stir vigorously to mix it in.

5 Warm the soup over a gentle heat for no more than 1–2 minutes. Any longer and the eggs may curdle. Serve immediately, with a plate of lemon quarters for those who wish to add extra juice.

Avgolemono has to be one of the most delicious and nourishing soups in the world. Its welcoming aroma always adds a bright note to a cold day, and it makes a very substantial meal by itself.

Lentil Soup Faki soupa

Serves 4

275g/10oz/1¼ cups brown-green
   lentils, preferably the small variety
150ml/¼ pint/⅔ cup extra virgin
   olive oil
1 onion, thinly sliced
2 garlic cloves, sliced into thin
   batons
1 carrot, sliced into thin discs
400g/14oz can chopped tomatoes
15ml/1 tbsp tomato purée (paste)
2.5ml/½ tsp dried oregano
1 litre/1¾ pints/4 cups hot water
salt and ground black pepper
30ml/2 tbsp roughly chopped fresh
   herb leaves, to garnish

*Lentils are a winter staple in
Greece and very delicious
they are too. As they do not
need soaking, they make an
easy option for a quick
meal. The secret of good
lentil soup is to be generous
with the olive oil. The soup
is served as a main meal,
accompanied by olives,
bread and cheese.*

1 Rinse the lentils, drain them and put them in a large pan with cold water to cover. Bring to the boil and boil for 3–4 minutes. Strain, discarding the liquid, and set the lentils aside.

2 Wipe the pan clean, heat the olive oil in it, then add the onion and sauté until translucent. Stir in the garlic, then, as soon as it becomes aromatic, return the lentils to the pan. Add the carrot, tomatoes, tomato purée and oregano. Stir in the hot water and a little pepper to taste.

3 Bring to the boil, then lower the heat, cover the pan and cook gently for 20–30 minutes until the lentils feel soft but have not begun to disintegrate. Add salt and the chopped herbs just before serving.

Cannellini Bean Soup Fasolia soupa

Serves 4

275g/10oz/1½ cups dried cannellini
   beans, soaked overnight in cold
   water
1 large onion, thinly sliced
1 celery stick, sliced
2–3 carrots, sliced in discs
400g/14oz can tomatoes
15ml/1 tbsp tomato purée (paste)
150ml/¼ pint/⅔ cup extra virgin
   olive oil
5ml/1 tsp dried oregano
30ml/2 tbsp finely chopped fresh
   flat-leaf parsley
salt and ground black pepper

*If there were one dish with
which the whole Greek
nation would identify, it
would be this one. It is
always served with bread
and olives, and perhaps raw
onion quarters. Pickled or
salted fish are also
traditional accompaniments.
For a more substantial meal
you could serve this soup
with fried squid.*

1 Drain the beans, rinse them under cold water and drain them again.
Tip them into a large pan, pour in enough water to cover and bring to
the boil. Cook for about 3 minutes, then drain.

2 Return the beans to the pan, pour in fresh water to cover them by
about 3cm/1¼in, then add the sliced onion, celery, carrots and tomatoes,
and stir in the tomato purée, olive oil and oregano. Season with a little
pepper, but don't add salt at this stage, as it would toughen the skins
of the beans.

3 Bring to the boil, lower the heat and cook for about 1 hour, until the
beans are just tender. Season with salt, stir in the parsley and serve.

Fried Courgettes and Aubergines with Tzatziki
Kolokythakia ke melitzanes me tzatziki

Serves 4

3 courgettes (zucchini)
1 aubergine (eggplant)
25g/1oz/¼ cup plain (all-purpose)
    flour
sunflower oil, for frying
salt and ground black pepper

For the tzatziki

15cm/6in piece of cucumber
200g/7oz Greek (US-strained plain)
    yogurt
1–2 garlic cloves, crushed
15ml/1 tbsp extra virgin olive oil
30ml/2 tbsp thinly sliced fresh mint
    leaves and mint sprigs, to garnish

1 Start by making the tzatziki. Peel the cucumber, grate it coarsely into a colander, then press out most of the liquid. Add the cucumber to the yogurt with the garlic, olive oil and mint. Stir in salt to taste, cover and chill in the refrigerator.

2 Trim the courgettes and aubergine, then rinse them and pat them dry with kitchen paper. Cut them lengthways into thin, long slices and toss them lightly in the flour.

3 Heat the oil in a large, heavy or non-stick frying pan and add as many courgette slices as the pan will hold in one layer. Cook for 1–2 minutes, until light golden, then turn them over and brown the other side. Lift the slices out, drain them on kitchen paper and keep them hot while cooking the remaining courgettes and then the aubergines.

4 Pile the fried slices in a large warmed bowl, sprinkle with salt and pepper and serve immediately with the bowl of chilled tzatziki garnished with a sprig of mint.

COOKS' TIP

If you are making the tzatziki several hours before serving, don't add the salt until later. If salt is added too far in advance, it will make the yogurt watery.

Tzatziki is a simple but very refreshing appetizer. It can be served with grilled meats and roasts, but its proper place is with freshly fried slices of courgettes and aubergines. When served with a salad, this dish makes the perfect first course for a dinner or a light lunch.

Half-moon Cheese Pies with Raisins and Pine Nuts Skaltsounakia

Makes 12–14

1 large (US extra large) egg, plus 1
    egg yolk for glazing
150g/5oz feta cheese
30ml/2 tbsp milk
30ml/2 tbsp chopped fresh mint
    leaves
15ml/1 tbsp raisins
15ml/1 tbsp pine nuts, lightly toasted
a little vegetable oil, for greasing

For the pastry

225g/8oz/2 cups self-raising (self-
    rising) flour
45ml/3 tbsp extra virgin olive oil
15g/½oz/1 tbsp butter, melted
90g/3½oz Greek (US-strained plain)
    yogurt

*These delicious small pies
always dazzle people. In
Crete, where they are very
popular, there are several
variations, including one
with a filling of sautéed wild
greens. Offer with drinks or
as part of a meze table.*

1 To make the pastry, put the flour in a bowl and mix in the oil, butter and yogurt by hand. Cover and rest in the refrigerator for 15 minutes.

2 Meanwhile, make the filling. Beat the egg lightly in a bowl. Crumble in the cheese, then mix in the milk, mint, raisins and pine nuts.

3 Preheat the oven to 190°C/375°F/Gas 5. Cover half of the pastry, thinly roll out the remainder and cut out 7.5cm/3in rounds.

4 Place a heaped teaspoon of filling on each round and fold the pastry over to make a half-moon shape. Press the edges to seal, then place the pies on a greased baking sheet. Repeat with the remaining pastry. Brush the pies with egg yolk and bake for 20 minutes, or until golden.

Feta and Roast Pepper Dip with Chillies
Htipiti

Serves 4

1 yellow or green elongated or
    bell-shaped (bell) pepper
1–2 fresh green chillies
200g/7oz feta cheese, cubed
60ml/4 tbsp extra virgin olive oil
juice of 1 lemon
45–60ml/3–4 tbsp milk
ground black pepper
a little finely chopped fresh flat-leaf
    parsley, to garnish
slices of toast, to serve

1 Scorch the pepper and chillies by threading them on metal skewers and turning them over a flame or under the grill (broiler), until charred all over.

2 Set the pepper and chillies aside until cool enough to handle. Peel off as much of their skin as possible and wipe the blackened bits off with kitchen paper. Slit the pepper and chillies and discard all the seeds and the stems.

3 Put the pepper and chilli flesh into a food processor. Add the other ingredients except the parsley and blend, adding a little more milk if too stiff. Spread on slices of toast, sprinkle a hint of chopped parsley on top, and serve.

This is a meze made famous in the beautiful city of Thessalonika. If you stop for an ouzo in the area called Lathathika, that used to be part of the old market, you will inevitably be served a small plate of htipiti. The dip is almost unknown elsewhere in Greece.

Stuffed Vine Leaves with Rice and Spring Herbs Dolmathes

1 If using fresh leaves, blanch them briefly in batches in a pan of boiling water, lifting them out with a slotted spoon after a few seconds and draining them in a colander. They should just be wilted to make them pliable; not cooked. Preserved leaves can be extremely salty and must be rinsed well before being immersed in a bowl of hot water. Leave the vine leaves in the water for 4–5 minutes, then drain them, rinse them and drain them again.

2 Put the rice in a large bowl and add the onions, spring onions, pine nuts, dill, mint and parsley. Mix well, then stir in half the olive oil and half the lemon juice. Season with salt and pepper and mix again.

3 Line the bottom of a wide pan with 2–3 of the vine leaves. Spread another vine leaf out on a board veined side up and place a heaped teaspoon of the stuffing near the stalk end. Fold the two opposite sides of the leaf over the stuffing and then roll up tightly from the stalk end. Make more dolmathes in the same way and pack them tightly together in circles in the pan.

4 Mix the remaining olive oil and lemon juice and pour the mixture over the dolmathes. Invert a small plate on top of the top layer to hold it down and prevent the rolls from unravelling. Carefully pour in the hot water, cover tightly and simmer gently for 1 hour. Serve the dolmathes hot or at room temperature. They look wonderful on a platter lined with fresh vine leaves, surrounded by the lemon wedges.

Serves 6

50 fresh or 225g/8oz preserved vine leaves
175g/6oz/scant 1 cup long grain rice
350g/12oz onions, very finely diced
4–5 spring onions (scallions), green and white parts, thinly sliced
30ml/2 tbsp pine nuts, toasted
60ml/4 tbsp finely chopped fresh dill
45ml/3 tbsp finely chopped fresh mint
30ml/2 tbsp finely chopped fresh flat-leaf parsley
150ml/¼ pint/⅔ cup extra virgin olive oil
juice of 1 lemon
450ml/¾ pint/scant 2 cups hot water
salt and ground black pepper
4–6 lemon wedges, to serve

These well-known and popular treats can be made with different stuffings and occasionally include meat. If fresh vine leaves are not available, look out for preserved ones in Greek grocers and some supermarkets.

Fried Squid Kalamarakia tiganita

1 Prepare the squid. Wash the squid thoroughly. Holding the body firmly, pull away the head and tentacles. If the ink sac is still intact, remove it and discard. Pull out the innards. Peel off and discard the thin purple skin on the body, but keep the two small fins on the sides. Slice the head across just under the eyes severing the tentacles. Discard the rest of the head. Squeeze the tentacles at the head end to push out the round beak in the centre. Throw this away. Rinse the bodies thoroughly, inside and out, then drain well. Slice the bodies into 3–4cm/1¼–1½in wide rings.

2 Season the flour with salt and pepper and put it in a large plastic bag. Add the squid, keeping the rings and tentacles separate, and toss until evenly coated. Shake off any excess flour.

3 Heat the oil in a large heavy or non-stick frying pan over a medium heat. When it is hot enough to sizzle, but is not smoking, add a batch of squid rings. They should fill the pan but not touch each other.

4 Let the squid rings cook for 2–3 minutes or until pale golden, then use a fork to turn each piece over. This is a laborious process but worthwhile. Let each ring cook for 1–2 minutes more, until pale golden, then lift out with a slotted spoon and drain on kitchen paper.

5 Continue to cook the squid, but leave the floured tentacles to last, and take care, as they spit spitefully. The tentacles will need very little cooking as the oil will have become quite hot and they will become crisp almost immediately. Turn them over after 1 minute and take them out as soon as they are crisp and golden all over.

6 Serve the fried squid on a large warmed platter and sprinkle some dried oregano on top. Surround the pieces with the lemon wedges and invite guests to squeeze a little lemon juice over each portion.

Serves 4

900g/2lb medium squid
50g/2oz/½ cup plain (all-purpose) flour
75ml/5 tbsp olive oil or sunflower oil, for frying
large pinch of dried oregano
salt and ground black pepper
1 lemon, quartered, to serve

There are few foods more appetizing than fried squid rolled in flour and shallow-fried. There's an art to this, as the olive oil has to be at precisely the right temperature to keep the squid tender and moist.

Baked Salt Cod with Potatoes, Tomatoes and Olives Bakaliaros plaki sto fourno

Serves 4

675g/1½lb salt cod
800g/1¾lb potatoes, peeled and cut
    into small wedges
1 large onion, finely chopped
2–3 garlic cloves, chopped
leaves from 1 fresh rosemary sprig
30ml/2 tbsp chopped fresh flat-leaf
    parsley
120ml/4fl oz/½ cup extra virgin
    olive oil
400g/14oz can chopped tomatoes
15ml/1 tbsp tomato purée (paste)
300ml/½ pint/1¼ cups hot water
5ml/1 tsp dried oregano
12 black olives
ground black pepper

1 Soak the cod in cold water overnight, changing the water as often as possible in the course of the evening and during the following day. The cod does not have to be skinned for this dish, but you should remove any obvious fins or bones.

2 Preheat the oven to 180°C/350°F/Gas 4. Mix the potatoes, onion, garlic, rosemary and parsley in a large roasting pan (tin). Grind in plenty of pepper. Add the olive oil and toss the mixture until well coated.

3 Drain the cod and cut it into serving pieces. Arrange the pieces of cod between the coated vegetables and spread the tomatoes over the surface. Stir the tomato purée into the hot water until dissolved, then pour the mixture over the contents of the pan. Sprinkle the oregano on top. Bake for 1 hour, basting occasionally with the pan juices.

4 Remove the roasting pan from the oven, sprinkle the olives on top, then cook it for 30 minutes more. Serve hot or cold, garnished with fresh herbs.

Salt cod is particularly popular in the spring, and the following dish is often on the menu at city restaurants on Fridays during Lent. Serve it with plenty of thickly sliced fresh bread, or serve cold, as part of the mezedes.

Grilled Swordfish Skewers
Xifias souvlakia

Serves 4

2 red onions, quartered
2 red or green (bell) peppers,
  quartered and seeded
20–24 thick cubes of swordfish,
  prepared weight 675–800g/
  1½–1¾lb
75ml/5 tbsp extra virgin olive oil
1 garlic clove, crushed
large pinch of dried oregano
salt and ground black pepper

1 Carefully separate the onion quarters in pieces, each composed of two or three layers. Slice each pepper quarter in half widthways.

2 Make the souvlakia by threading five or six pieces of swordfish on to each of four long metal skewers, alternating with pieces of the pepper and onion. Lay the souvlakia across a grill pan or roasting tray and set aside while you make the basting sauce.

3 Whisk the olive oil, garlic and oregano in a bowl. Add salt and pepper and whisk again. Brush the souvlakia generously on all sides with the basting sauce.

4 Preheat the grill (broiler) to the highest setting or prepare a barbecue. Slide the grill pan or roasting tray underneath the grill or transfer the skewers to the barbecue, making sure that they are not too close to the heat. Cook for 8–10 minutes, turning the skewers several times, until the fish is cooked and the peppers and onions have begun to scorch around the edges. Every time you turn the skewers, brush them with the basting sauce.

5 Serve the souvlakia immediately, with a fresh mixed salad.

Souvlakia are chunks of fish or meat that are threaded on long metal skewers, often with pieces of pepper and onions. The word is derived from souvla, the long metal spit that is inserted into a whole lamb or goat in order to spit-roast it over an open fire.Both meat and fish souvlakia are at their best when grilled over an open fire. They acquire an unmistakable smoky aroma that is irresistible.

Cuttlefish with Potatoes
Soupies me patates

1 Prepare the cuttlefish as for squid on page 29. Rinse and drain them well, then slice them in 2cm/¾in wide ribbons.

2 Heat the oil in a heavy pan, add the onion and sauté for about 5 minutes until light golden. Add the cuttlefish and sauté until all the water they exude has evaporated and the flesh starts to change colour. This will take 10–15 minutes.

3 Pour in the wine and, when it has evaporated, add the water. Cover and cook for 10 minutes, then add the potatoes, spring onions, lemon juice, and salt and pepper. There should be enough water to almost cover the ingredients; top up if necessary.

4 Cover and cook gently for 40 minutes or until the cuttlefish is tender, stirring occasionally. Add the dill and cook for 5 minutes. Serve hot.

**Serves 4 as a main course or
6 as a first course**
1kg/2¼lb fresh cuttlefish
150ml/¼ pint/⅔ cup extra virgin
    olive oil
1 large onion, about 225g/8oz,
    chopped
1 glass white wine, about 175ml/
    6fl oz/¾ cup
300ml/½ pint/1¼ cups hot water
500g/1¼lb potatoes, peeled and
    cubed
4–5 spring onions (scallions),
    chopped
juice of 1 lemon
60ml/4 tbsp chopped fresh dill
salt and ground black pepper

*Cuttlefish is sweeter and more tender than squid,
provided you buy small or medium-size specimens. If the
only ones available are very large, cook them for a little
longer than stated in the recipe. This wonderful dish is
often eaten during Lent.*

Hake with Spinach and Egg and Lemon Sauce
Bakaliaros me spanaki avgolemono

Serves 4

500g/1¼lb fresh spinach, trimmed
  of thick stalks
4 x 200g/7oz fresh hake steaks or 4
  pieces of cod fillet
30ml/2 tbsp plain (all-purpose) flour
75ml/5 tbsp extra virgin olive oil
1 glass white wine (175ml/6fl oz/
  ¾ cup)
3–4 strips of pared lemon rind
salt and ground black pepper

For the egg and lemon sauce

2 large (US extra large) eggs at room
  temperature
juice of ½ lemon
2.5ml/½ tsp cornflour (cornstarch)

1 Place the spinach leaves in a large pan with just the water that clings to the leaves after washing. Cover the pan and cook over a medium heat for 5–7 minutes. Remove the lid occasionally and turn the leaves using a wooden spoon. Drain and set the spinach aside.

2 Dust the fish lightly with the flour and shake off any excess. Heat the olive oil in a large frying pan, add the pieces of fish and sauté gently, for 2–3 minutes on each side, until the flesh starts to turn golden.

3 Pour the wine over the fish, add the lemon rind and some seasoning and carefully shake the pan from side to side to blend the flavourings. Lower the heat and simmer gently for a few minutes until the wine has reduced a little.

4 Add the spinach, distributing it evenly around the fish. Let it simmer for 3–4 minutes more, then pull the pan off the heat and let it stand for a few minutes before adding the sauce.

5 Prepare the egg and lemon sauce as described in the recipe for chicken soup with egg and lemon sauce (page 18), using the quantities listed here. Pour the sauce over the fish and spinach, place the pan over a very gentle heat and shake to amalgamate the ingredients. If it appears too dry add a little warm water. Allow to cook gently for 2–3 minutes and serve.

Fish cooked with greens has its roots in monastic life. Religious observance required that fish be eaten on certain holy days, such as Palm Sunday, and monastery cooks added interest to what might otherwise have been a bland meal, by including wild greens gathered from the hillsides.

Spring Lamb Casserole with Fresh Peas
Arnaki me araka

Serves 4–6

75ml/5 tbsp extra virgin olive oil
4–6 thick shoulder of lamb steaks,
  with the bone in
1 large onion, thinly sliced
5–6 spring onions (scallions),
  roughly chopped
2 carrots, sliced in rounds
juice of 1 lemon
1.2kg/2½lb fresh peas in pods,
  shelled (this will give you about
  500–675g/1¼–1½lb peas)
60ml/4 tbsp finely chopped fresh dill
salt and ground black pepper

1 Heat the oil in a wide, heavy pan. Brown the lamb on both sides. Lift out, then sauté the onion slices in the oil remaining in the pan until translucent. Add the spring onions and, 1 minute later, the carrots. Sauté for 3–4 minutes.

2 Return the lamb steaks to the pan, pour the lemon juice over them and let it evaporate for a few seconds. Pour over enough hot water to cover the meat. Add salt and pepper. Cover and simmer for 45–50 minutes, until the meat is almost tender, turning the steaks over and stirring the vegetables from time to time.

3 Add the peas and half the dill, with a little more water, if needed. Replace the lid and cook for 20–30 minutes until the meat and vegetables are fully cooked. Sprinkle the remaining dill over the casserole just before serving.

In Greece, milk-fed lamb is at its best in April and May, which is about the time when fresh peas put in an appearance in the markets. They are combined here to produce one of the most delicious Greek dishes – a real treat.

Grilled Skewered Lamb Arni souvlakia

1 Ask your butcher to trim the meat and cut it into 4cm/1½in cubes. A little fat is desirable with souvlakia, as it keeps them moist and succulent during cooking. Separate the onion quarters into pieces, each composed of two or three layers, and slice each pepper quarter in half widthways.

2 Put the oil, lemon juice, garlic and herbs in a large bowl. Season with salt and pepper and whisk well to combine. Add the meat cubes, stirring to coat them in the mixture.

3 Cover the bowl tightly and leave to marinate for 4–8 hours in the refrigerator, stirring several times.

4 Lift out the meat cubes, reserving the marinade, and thread them on long metal skewers, alternating each piece of meat with a piece of pepper and a piece of onion. Lay them across a grill pan or baking tray and brush them with the reserved marinade.

5 Preheat a grill (broiler) until hot or prepare a barbecue. Cook the souvlakia under a medium to high heat or over the hot coals for 10 minutes, until they start to get scorched. If using the grill, do not place them too close to the heat source. Turn the skewers over, brush them again with the marinade (or a little olive oil) and cook them for 10–15 minutes more. They should be served immediately.

COOK'S TIP
If you are barbecuing the souvlakia you may need to cook them for slightly longer, depending on the intensity of the heat.

This dish is street food par excellence. Lamb makes the best souvlakia, as there is nothing to match the succulence and flavour of barbecued lamb. Souvlakia are at their best served with tzatziki, chillies and salad.

Serves 4

1 small shoulder of lamb, boned and
  with most of the fat removed
2–3 onions, preferably red onions,
  quartered
2 red or green (bell) peppers,
  quartered and seeded
75ml/5 tbsp extra virgin olive oil
juice of 1 lemon
2 garlic cloves, crushed
5ml/1 tsp dried oregano
2.5ml/½ tsp dried thyme or some
  sprigs of fresh thyme
salt and ground black pepper

Spicy Sausage and Pepper Stew
Spetzofai pilioritiko

Serves 4

675g/1½lb long sweet peppers
75ml/5 tbsp extra virgin olive oil
500g/1¼lb spicy sausages (Italian
    garlic sausages, Merguez or
    Toulouse)
400g/14oz tomatoes, roughly sliced
5ml/1 tsp dried oregano or some
    fresh thyme, chopped
150ml/¼ pint/⅔ cup hot water
45ml/3 tbsp chopped flat-leaf parsley
salt and ground black pepper

1 Halve and seed the peppers and cut them into quarters. Heat the olive oil in a large heavy pan, add the peppers and sauté them over a medium heat for 10–15 minutes until they start to brown.

2 Meanwhile, slice the sausages into bitesize chunks. Carefully tip the hot olive oil into a frying pan. Add the sausages and fry them briefly, turning them frequently, to get rid of the excess fat but not to cook them. As soon as they are brown, remove the sausages from the pan with a slotted spoon and drain them on a plate lined with kitchen paper.

3 Add the tomatoes, sausages and herbs to the peppers. Stir in the water and season with salt and pepper, then cover the pan and cook gently for about 30 minutes. Mix in the parsley and serve.

VARIATION

If you prefer, you can stir in the parsley, spread the mixture in a medium baking dish and bake it in an oven preheated to 180°C/350°F/Gas 4. Cook for about 40 minutes, stirring occasionally and adding more hot water when needed.

This dish is a speciality of the Pelion, the beautiful mountain range that towers over the city of Volos on one side and the blue Aegean on the other, on the eastern coast of Greece. The peppers used traditionally in this recipe are the local thin, elongated yellow and green ones that are sweet. However, you can also use elongated red peppers or a mixture of the bell-shaped red, green and yellow peppers that are more commonly found.

Meat Rissoles with Cumin and Cracked Green Olives Soutzoukakia me elies

Serves 4

2–3 medium slices of bread, crusts removed
675g/1½lb/2½cups minced (ground) lamb or beef
2 garlic cloves, crushed
15ml/1 tbsp ground cumin
1 egg, lightly beaten
25g/1oz/¼ cup plain (all-purpose) flour
45ml/3 tbsp sunflower oil, for frying
salt and ground black pepper

For the sauce

45ml/3 tbsp olive oil
5ml/1 tsp cumin seeds
400g/14oz can chopped tomatoes
15ml/1 tbsp tomato purée (paste) diluted in 150ml/¼ pint/⅔ cup hot water
2.5ml/½ tsp dried oregano
12–16 green olives, preferably cracked ones, rinsed and drained

1 Soak the bread in water for 10 minutes, then drain, squeeze dry and place in a large bowl. Add the meat, garlic, cumin and egg. Season with salt and pepper, then mix either with a fork or your hands, until blended.

2 Take a small handful – the size of a large walnut – and roll it into a short, slim sausage. Set this aside. Continue until all the meat mixture has been used. Roll all the sausage-shaped rissoles lightly in flour, shaking each one to get rid of any excess.

3 Heat the oil in a large non-stick frying pan and fry the soutzoukakia, in batches if necessary, until they are golden on all sides. Lift them out and place them in a bowl. Discard the oil remaining in the pan.

4 Make the sauce. Heat the olive oil in a large pan. Add the cumin seeds and swirl them around for a few seconds until they are aromatic. Add the tomatoes and stir with a wooden spatula for about 2 minutes to break them up. Pour in the diluted tomato purée, mix well, then add the soutzoukakia. Stir in the oregano and olives, with salt and pepper to taste.

5 Spoon the sauce over the soutzoukakia, then cover and cook gently for 30 minutes, shaking the pan occasionally to prevent them from sticking. Tip into a warmed dish and serve.

This delicious dish is ideal for entertaining as it can be cooked in advance and re-heated as needed. Serve the rissoles (soutzoukakia) with plain rice, French fries or pasta.

Fried Meatballs
Keftethes

Serves 4

2 medium slices of bread, crusts
    removed
500g/1¼lb/2 cups minced (ground)
    lamb or beef
1 onion, grated
5ml/1 tsp each dried thyme and
    oregano
45ml/3 tbsp chopped fresh flat-leaf
    parsley, plus extra to garnish
1 egg, lightly beaten
25g/1oz/¼ cup plain (all-purpose)
    flour
30–45ml/2–3 tbsp vegetable oil
salt and ground black pepper
chopped fresh parsley and lemon
    wedges, to serve

*No Greek celebration is
complete without keftethes.
They are a must on the
meze table, as they are so
appetizing. Alternatively, they
make a luxurious addition to
a simple meal, such as a
warming soup.*

1 Soak the slices of bread in a bowl of water for about 10 minutes, then drain. With your hands, squeeze the bread dry before placing it in a large bowl.

2 Add the meat, onion, dried herbs, parsley, egg, salt and pepper to the bread. Mix together, preferably using your hands, until well blended.

3 Shape the meat mixture into walnut-size balls and roll the balls in the flour to lightly coat them, shaking off any excess.

4 Heat the oil in a large frying pan. When it is hot, add the meatballs and fry, turning them frequently, until they are cooked through and look crisp and brown all over. Lift out and drain on a double sheet of kitchen paper, to get rid of the excess oil. Sprinkle with chopped parsley and serve with lemon wedges.

Chicken Casserole with Olives
Kotopoulo me elies

Serves 4

75ml/5 tbsp extra virgin olive oil
1 organic or free-range chicken,
    about 1.6kg/3½lb, jointed
3–4 shallots, finely chopped
2 carrots, sliced
1 celery stick, roughly chopped
2 garlic cloves, chopped
juice of 1 lemon
300ml/½ pint/1¼ cups hot water
30ml/2 tbsp chopped flat-leaf parsley
12 black or green olives
salt and ground black pepper

1 Preheat the oven to 180°C/350°F/Gas 4. Heat the olive oil in a wide flameproof casserole and brown the chicken pieces on both sides. Lift them out and set them aside.

2 Add the shallots, carrots and celery to the oil remaining in the casserole and sauté them for a few minutes until the shallots are glistening. Stir in the garlic. As soon as it becomes aromatic, return the chicken to the pan and pour the lemon juice over the mixture. Let it bubble for a few minutes, then add the water and season with salt and pepper.

3 Cover the casserole and put it in the oven. Bake for 1 hour, turning the chicken pieces over occasionally. Remove the casserole from the oven, stir in the parsley and olives, mix well together, then re-cover the casserole and return it to the oven for about 30 minutes more

This is a very easy dish to prepare and cook but with its typical Mediterranean undertones it is also full of flavour. It is often served with French fries or plain boiled rice, but it goes equally well with boiled new potatoes.

Roast Chicken with Potatoes and Lemon
Kotopoulo fournou me patates

Serves 4

1 organic or free-range chicken,
   about 1.6kg/3½lb
2 garlic cloves, peeled, but left whole
15ml/1 tbsp chopped fresh thyme or
   oregano, or 5ml/1 tsp dried, plus
   2–3 fresh sprigs of thyme or
   oregano
800g/1¾lb potatoes
juice of 1 lemon
60ml/4 tbsp extra virgin olive oil
300ml/½ pint/1¼ cups hot water
salt and ground black pepper

1 Preheat the oven to 200°C/400°F/Gas 6. Place the chicken, breast side down, in a large roasting pan, then tuck the garlic cloves and the thyme or oregano sprigs inside the bird.

2 Peel the potatoes and quarter them lengthways. If they are very large, slice them lengthways into thinner pieces. Arrange the potatoes around the chicken, then pour the lemon juice over the chicken and potatoes. Season with salt and pepper, drizzle the olive oil over the top and add about three-quarters of the chopped fresh or dried thyme or oregano. Pour the hot water into the roasting pan.

3 Roast the chicken and potatoes for 30 minutes, then remove the roasting pan from the oven and carefully turn the chicken over. Season the bird with a little more salt and pepper, sprinkle over the remaining fresh or dried herbs, and add more hot water, if needed. Reduce the oven temperature to 190°C/375°F/Gas 5.

4 Return the chicken and potatoes to the oven and roast them for another hour, or slightly longer, by which time both the chicken and the potatoes will be a golden colour. Serve with a crisp leafy salad.

This is a lovely, easy dish for a family meal. As with other Greek roasts, everything is baked together so that the potatoes absorb all the different flavours, especially that of the lemon.

Giant Beans Baked with Tomatoes Gigantes fournou

1 Place the beans in a large bowl, cover with plenty of cold water, then leave the beans to soak overnight. The next day, drain the beans, then rinse them under cold water and drain again. Tip the beans into a large pan, pour in plenty of water to cover, then bring to the boil. Cover the pan and cook the beans until they are almost tender. Gigantes are not like other beans – they cook quickly, so keep testing the beans after they have cooked for 30–40 minutes. They should not be allowed to disintegrate from overcooking.

2 When the beans are cooked, tip them into a colander to drain, discarding the cooking liquid, then set them aside. Preheat the oven to 180°C/350°F/Gas 4.

3 Heat the olive oil in the clean pan, add the onions and sauté until light golden. Add the celery, carrots, garlic and dried herbs and stir with a wooden spatula until the garlic becomes aromatic.

4 Stir in the tomatoes, cover and cook for 10 minutes. Pour in the diluted tomato purée, then return the beans to the pan. Stir in the sugar and parsley, with plenty of salt and pepper.

5 Tip the bean mixture into a baking dish and bake for 30 minutes, checking the beans once or twice and adding more hot water if they look dry. The surface should be slightly scorched and sugary.

Gigantes are a type of white bean, resembling butter beans, but larger, rounder and much sweeter. They come from the north of Greece and the best come from Kastoria. Similar beans are found in Italy and Spain. In major cities outside Greece, look for them in specialist food stores.

Serves 6

400g/14oz/1¾ cups Greek fasolia gigantes or similar large dried white beans
150ml/¼ pint/⅔ cup extra virgin olive oil
2–3 onions, total weight about 300g/11oz, chopped
1 celery stick, thinly sliced
2 carrots, cubed
3 garlic cloves, thinly sliced
5ml/1 tsp each dried oregano and thyme
400g/14oz can chopped tomatoes
30ml/2 tbsp tomato purée (paste) diluted in 300ml/½ pint/1¼ cups hot water
2.5ml/½ tsp granulated (white) sugar
45ml/3 tbsp finely chopped flat-leaf parsley
salt and ground black pepper

Aubergines Baked with Tomatoes and Cheese
Melitzanes sto fourno

Serves 4

4 large aubergines (eggplant), total
    weight about 1.2kg/2½lb
150ml/¼ pint/⅔ cup sunflower oil
50g/2oz/½ cup freshly grated
    Parmesan or Cheddar cheese

For the sauce

45ml/3 tbsp extra virgin olive oil
2 garlic cloves, crushed
2 x 400g/14oz cans tomatoes
5ml/1 tsp tomato purée (paste)
2.5ml/½ tsp sugar
2.5ml/½ tsp dried oregano
30–45ml/2–3 tbsp chopped fresh
    flat-leaf parsley
salt and ground black pepper

*This is a delectable dish,
particularly when made in
the middle of summer
when the aubergines are
at their sweetest.*

1 Trim the aubergines and cut lengthways into 1cm/½in thick slices. Heat the oil in a large frying pan and fry the slices briefly in batches. Lift out when they are golden on both sides and drain on kitchen paper.

2 Arrange the aubergine slices in two layers in a baking dish. Sprinkle with salt and pepper.

3 Make the sauce. Heat the oil gently in a large pan, add the garlic and sauté for a few seconds, then add the tomatoes, tomato purée, sugar and oregano and season to taste. Cover and simmer for 25–30 minutes or until the sauce is thick and velvety, stirring occasionally. Stir in the parsley and cook for 2–3 minutes.

4 Meanwhile, preheat the oven to 180°C/350°F/ Gas 4. Spread the sauce over the aubergines to cover them. Sprinkle the cheese on top and bake for 40 minutes.

Cabbage Salad with Lemon Vinaigrette and Black Olives Lahano salata

Serves 4
1 white cabbage
12 black olives

For the vinaigrette
75–90ml/5–6 tbsp extra virgin olive
    oil
30ml/2 tbsp lemon juice
1 garlic clove, crushed
30ml/2 tbsp finely chopped fresh
    flat-leaf parsley
salt

This delightful salad is made with compact creamy-coloured 'white' cabbage. It produces a rather sweet tasting, unusual salad, which has a crisp and refreshing texture.

1 Cut the cabbage in quarters, discard the outer leaves and tim off any thick, hard stems as well as the hard base.

2 Lay each quarter in turn on its side and cut long, very thin slices until you reach the central core, which should be discarded. The key to a perfect cabbage salad is to shred the cabbage as finely as possible. Place the shredded cabbage in a bowl and stir in the black olives.

3 Make the vinaigrette by whisking the olive oil, lemon juice, garlic, parsley and salt together in a bowl until well blended. Pour the dressing over the salad, and toss the cabbage and olives until everything is evenly coated with the vinaigrette.

Potato and Feta Salad
Patates salata me feta

1 Bring a pan of lightly salted water to the boil and cook the potatoes in their skins for 25–30 minutes, until tender. Take care not to let them become soggy and disintegrate. Drain them thoroughly and let them cool a little.

2 When the potatoes are cool enough to handle, peel them and place in a large bowl. If they are very small, keep them whole; otherwise cut them in large cubes. Add the spring onions, capers, olives, feta and fresh herbs and toss gently to mix.

3 To make the vinaigrette, place the oil in a bowl with the lemon juice and anchovies. Whisk thoroughly until the dressing emulsifies and thickens. Whisk in the yogurt, dill and mustard, with salt and pepper to taste.

4 Dress the salad while the potatoes are still warm, tossing lightly to coat everything in the delicious anchovy vinaigrette.

COOK'S TIP
The salad tastes better if it has had time to sit for an hour or so at room temperature and absorb all the flavours before it is served. Any leftover salad will be delicious the next day, but take it out of the refrigerator about an hour before it is to be served or the flavours will be dulled.

Serves 4
500g/1¼lb small new potatoes
5 spring onions (scallions), green and
    white parts, finely chopped
15ml/1 tbsp rinsed bottled capers
8–10 black olives
115g/4oz feta cheese, cut into small
    cubes
45ml/3 tbsp finely chopped fresh
    flat-leaf parsley
30ml/2 tbsp finely chopped fresh
    mint

For the vinaigrette
90–120ml/6–8 tbsp extra virgin olive
    oil
juice of 1 lemon, or to taste
2 salted or preserved anchovies,
    rinsed and finely chopped
45ml/3 tbsp Greek (US-strained
    plain) yogurt
45ml/3 tbsp finely chopped fresh dill
5ml/1 tsp French mustard
salt and ground black pepper

A potato salad may sound mundane but this one is not, as it is redolent with the aromas of the herbs and has layer upon layer of flavours. It is an easy dish to assemble, so makes a perfect lunch or dinner for a busy day.

Cauliflower with Egg and Lemon Sauce
Kounoupithi avgolemono

Serves 6

75–90ml/5–6 tbsp extra virgin olive
  oil
1 medium cauliflower, divided into
  large florets
2 eggs
juice of 1 lemon
5ml/1 tsp cornflour (cornstarch),
  mixed to a cream with a little cold
  water
30ml/2 tbsp chopped fresh flat-leaf
  parsley
salt

1 Heat the olive oil in a large heavy pan, add the cauliflower florets and sauté over a medium heat until they start to brown.

2 Pour in enough hot water to almost cover the cauliflower, add salt to taste, then cover the pan and cook for 7–8 minutes until the florets are just soft. Remove the pan from the heat and leave to stand, covered, while you make the sauce.

3 Beat the eggs in a bowl, add the lemon juice and cornflour and beat until well mixed. While beating, add a few tablespoons of the hot liquid from the cauliflower. Pour the egg mixture slowly over the cauliflower, then stir gently. Place the pan over a very gentle heat for 2 minutes to thicken the sauce. Spoon into a warmed serving bowl, sprinkle the chopped parsley over the top and serve.

Cauliflower has a bit of a bad image but, if you treat it well, it can be quite delicious. In Greece it is very popular and is used in a number of different ways. Here it is teamed with a lemon sauce. Try serving it with something rich and appetizing, such as keftethes (fried meatballs).

Fresh Green Beans with Tomato Sauce
Fasolakia

Serves 4

800g/1¾lb green beans, trimmed
150ml/¼ pint/⅔ cup extra virgin olive
    oil
1 large onion, thinly sliced
2 garlic cloves, chopped
2 small potatoes, peeled and cubed
675g/1½lb tomatoes or a
    400g/14oz can plum tomatoes,
    chopped
150ml/¼ pint/⅔ cup hot water
45–60ml/3–4 tbsp chopped fresh
    parsley
salt and ground black pepper

*This dish is made with
different kinds of fresh
beans according to what is
available. When the beans
are tender and the tomatoes
sweet, the dish, although
frugal, can have an
astoundingly good flavour.
It is usually accompanied
by feta cheese and fresh
crusty bread.*

1 If the beans are very long, cut them in half. Drop them into a bowl of cold water.

2 Heat the olive oil in a large pan, add the onion and sauté until translucent. Add the garlic, then, when it becomes aromatic, stir in the potatoes and sauté the mixture for a few minutes.

3 Add the tomatoes, with the hot water and cook for 5 minutes. Drain the beans, rinse them and drain again, then add them to the pan with a little salt and pepper to season. Cover and simmer for 30 minutes. Stir in the chopped parsley, with a little more hot water if the mixture looks dry. Cook for 10 minutes more, until the beans are very tender. Serve hot with slices of feta cheese, if you like.

Walnut Cake Karythopitta

1 Preheat the oven to 190°C/375°F/Gas 5. Grease a 35 x 23cm/14 x 9in roasting pan (tin) or baking dish that is at least 5cm/2in deep. Cream the butter in a large mixing bowl until soft, then add the sugar and beat well until the mixture is light and fluffy.

2 Add the egg yolks one by one, beating the mixture after each addition. Stir in the brandy and cinnamon. Coarsely chop the walnuts in a food processor and add them to the mixture. Mix in the walnuts using a wooden spoon. Do not use an electric mixer at this stage.

3 Sift the flour with the baking powder and set aside. Whisk the egg whites with a pinch of salt until they are stiff. Fold them into the creamed mixture, alternating with tablespoons of flour until they and the flour have all been incorporated.

4 Spread the mixture evenly in the prepared pan or dish. It should be about 4cm/1½in deep. Bake for about 40 minutes, until the top is golden and a skewer inserted in the cake comes out clean. Take the cake out of the oven and let it rest in the pan or dish while you make the syrup.

5 Mix the sugar and 300ml/½ pint/1¼ cups water in a small pan. Heat gently, stirring, until the sugar has dissolved. Bring to the boil, lower the heat and add the brandy, orange rind and cinnamon sticks. Simmer for 10 minutes.

6 Slice the karythopitta into 6cm/2½in diamond or square shapes while still hot and strain the syrup slowly over it. Let it stand for 10–20 minutes until it has absorbed the syrup and is thoroughly soaked.

This luscious cake is the finest Greek dessert of all. Its honey-soft texture, coupled with the sweetness of the walnuts, makes it irresistible. Perfect for a large party, the cake tastes even better the day after it has been made.

Serves 10–12

150g/5oz/⅔ cup unsalted (sweet) butter
115g/4oz/½ cup caster (superfine) sugar
4 eggs, separated
60ml/4 tbsp brandy
2.5ml/½ tsp ground cinnamon
300g/11oz/2¾ cups shelled walnuts
150g/5oz/1¼ cups self-raising (self-rising) flour
5ml/1 tsp baking powder
salt

For the syrup

250g/9oz/generous 1 cup caster (superfine) sugar
30ml/2 tbsp brandy
2–3 strips of pared orange rind
2 cinnamon sticks

Semolina Cake Halvas

Serves 6–8

500g/1¼lb/2½ cups caster
(superfine) sugar
1 litre/1¾ pints/4 cups cold water
1 cinnamon stick
250ml/8fl oz/1 cup olive oil
350g/12oz/2 cups coarse semolina
50g/2oz/½ cup blanched almonds
30ml/2 tbsp pine nuts
5ml/1 tsp ground cinnamon

1 Put the sugar in a heavy pan, pour in the water and add the cinnamon stick. Bring to the boil, stirring until the sugar dissolves, then boil without stirring for about 4 minutes to make a syrup.

2 Meanwhile, heat the oil in a separate, heavy pan. When it is almost smoking, add the semolina gradually and stir continuously until it turns light brown.

3 Lower the heat, add the almonds and pine nuts and brown together for 2–3 minutes, stirring continuously. Take the semolina mixture off the heat and set aside. Remove the cinnamon stick from the hot syrup using a slotted spoon and discard it.

4 Protecting your hand with an oven glove or dishtowel, carefully add the hot syrup to the semolina mixture, stirring all the time. The mixture will hiss and spit at this point, so stand well away from it.

5 Return the pan to a gentle heat and stir until all the syrup has been absorbed and the mixture looks smooth. Remove the pan from the heat, cover it with a clean dishtowel and let it stand for 10 minutes so that any remaining moisture is absorbed.

6 Scrape the mixture into a 20–23cm/8–9in round cake tin (pan), preferably fluted, and set it aside. When it is cold, unmould it on to a platter and dust it all over with the ground cinnamon.

Halvas is the universal family treat, loved by everyone in Greece. It takes very little time to make – about 20 minutes – and uses quite inexpensive ingredients that every Greek household routinely has. It makes a perfect accompaniment to Greek coffee.

Christmas Honey Cookies Melomakarona

Makes 20

2.5ml/½ tsp bicarbonate of soda (baking soda)
grated rind and juice of 1 large orange
150ml/¼ pint/⅔ cup extra virgin olive oil
75g/3oz/6 tbsp caster (superfine) sugar
60ml/4 tbsp brandy
7.5ml/1½ tsp ground cinnamon
400g/14oz/3½ cups self-raising (self-rising) flour sifted with a pinch of salt
115g/4oz/1 cup shelled walnuts, chopped

For the syrup

225g/8oz/1 cup clear honey
115g/4oz/½ cup caster (superfine) sugar

A classic festive treat, Christmas would lose some of its lustre without honey-coated melomakarona.

1 Mix together the baking soda and orange juice. Beat the oil and sugar until blended. Beat in the brandy and 2.5ml/½ tsp of the cinnamon, then the orange juice and soda. Using your hand, gradually work the flour and salt into the mixture. As soon as it becomes possible to do so, knead it. Add the orange rind and knead until the dough is pliable.

2 Preheat the oven to 180°C/350°F/Gas 4. Flour your hands and pinch off small pieces of the dough. Shape them into 6cm/2½in long ovals and place on ungreased baking sheets. Flatten each cookie a little. Bake for 25 minutes, until golden. Cool, then transfer to a wire rack to harden.

3 Meanwhile, make the syrup. Place the honey, sugar and 150ml/¼ pint/⅔ cup water in a small pan. Bring gently to the boil, skim, then lower the heat and simmer for 5 minutes. Immerse the cookies about six at a time into the hot syrup and leave them for 1–2 minutes.

4 Lift them out with a slotted spoon and place on a platter in a single layer. Sprinkle with the walnuts and remaining cinnamon.

Nutritional notes

Chicken Soup: Energy 96kcal/404kJ; Protein 3.3g; Carbohydrate 10.9g, of which sugars 0.2g; Fat 4.7g, of which saturates 1.2g; Cholesterol 151mg; Calcium 39mg; Fibre 0.4g; Sodium 10mg.

Lentil Soup: Energy 462kcal/1935kJ; Protein 18.4g; Carbohydrate 40g, of which sugars 6.6g; Fat 26.6g, of which saturates 3.7g; Cholesterol 0mg; Calcium 86mg; Fibre 8g; Sodium 64mg.

Cannellini Bean Soup: Energy 490kcal/2051kJ; Protein 17.9g; Carbohydrate 47.8g, of which sugars 11.3g; Fat 26.6g, of which saturates 4.1g; Cholesterol 0mg; Calcium 89mg; Fibre 8.4g; Sodium 45mg.

Fried Courgettes and Aubergines with Tzatziki: Energy 247kcal/1020kJ; Protein 7.6g; Carbohydrate 11g, of which sugars 5.5g; Fat 19.9g, of which saturates 4.6g; Cholesterol 0mg; Calcium 149mg; Fibre 3.2g; Sodium 41mg.

Half-moon Cheese Pies: Energy 160kcal/669kJ; Protein 5g; Carbohydrate 16.4g, of which sugars 2.5g; Fat 8.8g, of which saturates 3.4g; Cholesterol 31mg; Calcium 129mg; Fibre 0.7g; Sodium 270mg.

Feta and Roast Pepper Dip: Energy 245kcal/1014kJ; Protein 8.7g; Carbohydrate 4.5g, of which sugars 4.3g; Fat 21.5g, of which saturates 8.6g; Cholesterol 36mg; Calcium 198mg; Fibre 0.8g; Sodium 727mg.

Stuffed Vine Leaves: Energy 188kcal/782kJ; Protein 2.9g; Carbohydrate 13.6g, of which sugars 4.1g; Fat 11.3g, of which saturates 1.3g; Cholesterol 0mg; Calcium 37mg; Fibre 1.4g; Sodium 9mg.

Fried Squid: Energy 349kcal1464kJ; Protein 35.8g; Carbohydrate 12.4g, of which sugars 0.2g; Fat 17.7g, of which saturates 2.9g; Cholesterol 506mg; Calcium 47mg; Fibre 0.4g; Sodium 248mg.

Baked Salt Cod: Energy 624kcal/1624kJ; Protein 61g; Carbohydrate 45.6g, of which sugars 12.9g; Fat 23.3g, of which saturates 3.5g; Cholesterol 100mg; Calcium 98mg; Fibre 4.8g; Sodium 918mg.

Swordfish Skewers: Energy 363kcal/1511kJ; Protein 32.2g; Carbohydrate 11.5g, of which sugars 9.6g; Fat 21.2g, of which saturates 3.6g; Cholesterol 69mg; Calcium 33mg; Fibre 2.5g; Sodium 225mg.

Cuttlefish with Potatoes: Energy 540kcal/2254kJ; Protein 43.3g; Carbohydrate 24.7g, of which sugars 5.1g; Fat 27.3g, of which saturates 4.2g; Cholesterol 274mg; Calcium 176mg; Fibre 2.2g; Sodium 943mg.

Hake with Spinach and Egg and Lemon Sauce: Energy 441kcal/1839kJ; Protein 43.6g; Carbohydrate 10.6g, of which sugars 2.3g; Fat 22.1g, of which saturates 3.5g; Cholesterol 141mg; Calcium 273mg; Fibre 2.9g; Sodium 413mg.

Spring Lamb Casserole: Energy 858kcal/3551kJ; Protein 40.2g; Carbohydrate 29g, of which sugars 11.8g; Fat 65.6g, of which saturates 26.9g; Cholesterol 119mg; Calcium 79mg; Fibre 10.2g; Sodium 132mg.

Grilled Skewered Lamb: Energy 415kcal/1724kJ; Protein 31.2g; Carbohydrate 9.6g, of which sugars 8.1g; Fat 28.2g, of which saturates 8.8g; Cholesterol 138mg; Calcium 31mg; Fibre 2.1g; Sodium 86mg.

Spicy Sausage and Pepper Stew: Energy 573kcal/2378kJ; Protein 14.8g; Carbohydrate 28.9g, of which sugars 15.9g; Fat 45g, of which saturates 14.7g; Cholesterol 50mg; Calcium 106mg; Fibre 5g; Sodium 1033mg.

Meat Rissoles: Energy 625kcal/2602kJ; Protein 37.3g; Carbohydrate 18.5g, of which sugars 4.3g; Fat 45.2g, of which saturates 13.8g; Cholesterol 178mg; Calcium 98mg; Fibre 2.7g; Sodium 1101mg.

Fried Meatballs: Energy 375kcal/1565kJ; Protein 27.7g; Carbohydrate 13g, of which sugars 1.6g; Fat 24g, of which saturates 8.8g; Cholesterol 144mg; Calcium 78mg; Fibre 1.2g; Sodium 178mg.

Chicken Casserole with Olives: Energy 726kcal/3008kJ; Protein 54.9g; Carbohydrate 3.8g, of which sugars 3.5g; Fat 54.5g, of which saturates 13.1g; Cholesterol 289mg; Calcium 55mg; Fibre 1.9g; Sodium 435mg.

Roast Chicken: Energy 767kcal/3195kJ; Protein 53.3g; Carbohydrate 32.5g, of which sugars 2.9g; Fat 47.7g, of which saturates 11.8g; Cholesterol 264mg; Calcium 51mg; Fibre 2.6g; Sodium 206mg.

Giant Beans with Tomatoes: Energy 562kcal/2358kJ; Protein 24.8g; Carbohydrate 58.5g, of which sugars 14.9g; Fat 27.2g, of which saturates 3.9g; Cholesterol 0mg; Calcium 167mg; Fibre 19.8g; Sodium 68mg.

Aubergines Baked with Tomatoes and Cheese: Energy 441kcal/1830kJ; Protein 9.6g; Carbohydrate 13.6g, of which sugars 13g; Fat 39.3g, of which saturates 7.3g; Cholesterol 13mg; Calcium 218mg; Fibre 8.7g; Sodium 173mg.

Cabbage Salad with Lemon Vinaigrette and Black Olives: Energy 208kcal/861kJ; Protein 4g; Carbohydrate 12.9g, of which sugars 12.5g; Fat 15.8g, of which saturates 2.2g; Cholesterol 0mg; Calcium 155mg; Fibre 6.2g; Sodium 303mg.

Potato and Feta Salad: Energy 138kcal/566kJ; Protein 1.3g; Carbohydrate 1.2g, of which sugars 1.1g; Fat 14.2g, of which saturates 2g; Cholesterol 0mg; Calcium 75mg; Fibre 1.4g; Sodium 40mg.

Cauliflower with Egg and Lemon Sauce: Energy 211kcal/874kJ; Protein 8g; Carbohydrate 5.2g, of which sugars 3.4g; Fat 17.8g, of which saturates 3g; Cholesterol 95mg; Calcium 63mg; Fibre 2.8g; Sodium 51mg.

Fresh Green Beans with Tomato Sauce: Energy 350kcal/1448kJ; Protein 6.6g; Carbohydrate 21.9g, of which sugars 13.4g; Fat 26.9g, of which saturates 4g; Cholesterol 0mg; Calcium 121mg; Fibre 7.7g; Sodium 25mg.

Walnut Cake: Energy 563kcal/2349kJ; Protein 8.5g; Carbohydrate 50.6g, of which sugars 39.2g; Fat 35.3g, of which saturates 10.1g; Cholesterol 108mg; Calcium 114mg; Fibre 1.5g; Sodium 177mg.

Semolina Cake: Energy 888kcal/3731kJ; Protein 9.1g; Carbohydrate 133.1g, of which sugars 87.6g; Fat 39.1g, of which saturates 4.9g; Cholesterol 0mg; Calcium 75mg; Fibre 1.9g; Sodium 13mg.

Christmas Honey Cookies: Energy 173kcal/724kJ; Protein 2.7g; Carbohydrate 19.5g, of which sugars 4.6g; Fat 9.2g, of which saturates 1.1g; Cholesterol 0mg; Calcium 78mg; Fibre 0.8g; Sodium 73mg.

Index